101 Tips
for Simplifying Diabetes

The University of New Mexico
Diabetes Care Team

American Diabetes Association

*Cure • Care • Commitment*SM

RC
660.4
.A155
2001

Director, Book Publishing	John Fedor
Book Acquisitions	Sherrye Landrum
Editor	Abe Ogden
Production Manager	Peggy M. Rote
Composition	Circle Graphics, Inc.
Cover Design	Bremmer & Goris
Printer	Transcontinental Printing

Printed in Canada
1 3 5 7 9 10 8 6 4 2

ADA titles may be purchased for business or promotional use or for special sales. For information, please write to Lee Romano Sequeira, Special Sales & Promotions, at the address below.

American Diabetes Association
1701 North Beauregard Street
Alexandria, Virginia 22311

Library of Congress Cataloging-in-Publication Data

101 tips for simplifying diabetes / University of New Mexico Diabetes Care Team.
     p. cm.
  Includes index.
  ISBN 1-58040-047-7 (alk. paper)
     1. Diabetes—Popular works.   2. Diabetes—Miscellanea.
  I. Title: One hundred and one tips for simplifying diabetes.
  II. Title: One hundred one tips for simplifying diabetes.
  III. University of New Mexico. Diabetes Care Team.
  IV. American Diabetes Association.
  RC660.4 .A155 2001
  616.4'62—dc21

                            2001046105

101 TIPS FOR SIMPLIFYING DIABETES

▼

TABLE OF CONTENTS

ACKNOWLEDGMENTS

▼

The University of New Mexico Diabetes Care Team wishes to acknowledge the graphic design and editorial assistance of Carolyn King, M.Ed., of the University of New Mexico for her help with this book. We also acknowledge the editorial assistance of Sherrye Landrum of the American Diabetes Association. Thanks to Abe Ogden for copyediting this book and to Dr. James Gavin for reviewing the manuscript.

INTRODUCTION

▼

This is our third book in the American Diabetes Association *101 Tips* book series. We began this series in 1995 and are pleased with the positive response our book received from people with diabetes. Since that time, other expert groups have contributed books to the series that proved to be just as popular. Why has this series been so well-received? We believe that there are two main reasons. First, the information is presented in a clear, easy-to-read format so the reader knows exactly what we're saying. Second, and most important, people with diabetes realize that the key to good living with diabetes depends upon preventing the complications of this disease. In many ways, diabetes is a "do it yourself" disease. Complications can only be prevented when you make the correct decisions concerning your health care. The Diabetes Healthcare Team can help you with this, but the real key to your future is how you use the knowledge you gain from books, magazines, the Internet, etc. We hope this book and the others in this series will assist you in taking charge of your diabetes and support your quest for a healthier and happier life.

The University of New Mexico Diabetes Care Team
David S. Schade, M.D.
Mark R. Burge, M.D.
Leslie Atler, Ph.D.
Lisa Butler, B.U.S.
Lynda Shey, R.N., C.D.E.

Chapter 1
WHIPPING YOUR BLOOD
SUGARS INTO SHAPE

*C*an one low blood sugar put me at risk for another one?

TIP:

Frequent episodes of hypoglycemia (low blood sugar) can cause a problem called hypoglycemia unawareness. This is a condition in which the warning signs of hypoglycemia (shaking, sweating, or nervousness) don't show up until your blood sugar is so low that you can't correct the problem by yourself. Hypoglycemia unawareness is a serious problem and can seriously limit your diabetes care team's ability to meet your treatment goals. Recent research has shown that if you have two low blood sugars within 24 hours, it's much harder (or even impossible) to recognize the second episode. This is because your body's hormone response to the first episode of hypoglycemia reduces your body's hormone response to the second episode. Thus, you are at a higher risk for a severe low blood sugar for about 24 hours after experiencing an episode of hypoglycemia. One way to prevent hypoglycemia unawareness is to avoid hypoglycemia for several days or a week. Then your body will be better prepared to recognize a low blood sugar attack.

*S*hould I eat before I drive my car?

▼
TIP:

For years, researchers have tried to determine what a good blood sugar level is for someone who is going to drive a car or operate any type of heavy machinery. Until recently, the answer was unclear. A new study tried to shed light on this issue by having 37 people with type 1 diabetes operate an advanced driving simulator while various levels of insulin and glucose were injected into their veins. The patients did not know what their blood sugar level was. Driving ability was studied at four different blood sugar levels: 110 mg/dl (normal), 65 mg/dl, 56 mg/dl, and less than 50 mg/dl. Surprisingly, the patients did not recognize that they were hypoglycemic until their blood sugars were less than 50 mg/dl. However, their driving performance was worse at every level of low blood sugar when compared to the normal blood sugar test. Thus, driving ability suffered even before the patients noticed that they had low blood sugar. With this in mind, you should always determine your blood sugar level before you drive a car. If your blood sugar is below 80 mg/dl, eat a snack to avoid impaired driving ability.

Specialist   Generalist

If I am hospitalized with diabetic ketoacidosis, should I be under the care of a diabetes specialist?

▼
TIP:

For decades, the medical community has debated over who can give you the best care—a specialist or your general care physician. In debates like this, it's hard to come up with a clear answer. Often, the best solution is a mix of both. Recently, a study examined the outcome of patients who were hospitalized for diabetic keto-acidosis. They compared the care received from a general physician and an endocrinologist, a doctor who specializes in hormone diseases, including diabetes. Patients who received care from an endocrinologist had shorter hospital stays (3.3 days versus 4.9 days), lower hospital bills ($5,400 versus $10,100), and had to readmit themselves to the hospital less (2% versus 6%). Although there was no difference in death rates or complication rates between the endocrinologists and the generalists, the numbers suggest that endocrinologists are able to care for diabetic ketoacidosis more effectively in terms of time and money. However, just because you visit a specialist doesn't mean you can't still receive care from your general physician. If a diabetes specialist is available, try to coordinate the care you receive from them with the care you receive from your generalist. Working as a team will provide the best results.

*H*ow can sticking my finger for a blood
sample be less painful?

▼
TIP:

There are several ways to make getting a drop of blood less
painful.

- Do not swab your finger with alcohol. It stings, and it's not
  necessary.
- The tip of your finger is the most sensitive part. The side of your
  fingertip is less sensitive and is a better place to stick.
- "Milking" your finger for blood (squeezing your finger several
  times after you stick it) can be uncomfortable. Instead, make a
  puncture deep enough so that you don't need to squeeze your
  finger after the stick to get enough blood for the sample.
- Another trick is to trap extra blood in your finger before sticking
  it. Use the thumb of the same hand you're using to get the blood
  sample from. Slide your thumb from the base of your finger up
  to the last joint. This makes more blood available by pushing
  extra blood up into your fingertip. Also, you might try crowding
  your fingertips together. If your fingertip gets redder, there's
  more blood than usual. This makes it easier to get a drop of
  blood.
- Use another site besides the finger. See tip on page 83 for more.

*H*ow long does it take me to recover from
an episode of severe hypoglycemia?

▼
TIP:

L ow blood sugars can affect your ability to think clearly, because
your brain does not work normally when it's not receiving
enough sugar. The good news is that your brain function usually
returns to normal after your low blood sugar is treated. Studies have
shown that if you're practicing intensive diabetes management,
frequent hypoglycemia does not cause any permanent brain damage.
Researchers recently studied brain function before and after severe
hypoglycemia. They found that brain function generally returns to
normal within 36 hours of a severe hypoglycemic attack. However,
they also found that patients with frequent hypoglycemia were more
likely to suffer from extreme mood changes, such as depression,
though whether or not frequent hypoglycemia causes these changes
is still unclear. You should also be aware that prolonged or severe
hypoglycemia that is untreated can cause permanent brain damage
or lead to a coma.

Why don't I wake up when my blood sugar gets low at night?

▼
TIP:

Hypoglycemia (low blood sugar) that hits while you sleep can be a serious problem. In fact, many people with diabetes are so afraid of an overnight attack they let their diabetes management slip. Their fear is understandable. Researchers have found that sleep can interfere with your body's normal response to hypoglycemia. Normally, when you have a low blood sugar, your body releases hormones that raise the blood sugar. Epinephrine (or adrenaline) is probably the most important of these chemicals. While you sleep, the epinephrine responses to hypoglycemia can be a lot lower than when you're awake, which might be why you don't wake up during the night if your blood sugar drops too low. If you think you are experiencing hypoglycemia during the night, you should set your alarm clock for 3:00 a.m. so you can check your blood sugar in the middle of the night. If your blood sugar is below 65 mg/dl, you should lower your nighttime insulin dose or take a bedtime snack in order to prevent hypoglycemia. You might also be able to change the kind of insulin you take to reduce nighttime low blood sugars.

*H*ow can I help someone who has low
blood sugar?

▼
TIP:

B e prepared. Low blood sugar can make people feel very irrita-
ble. Very low blood sugars can make it almost impossible to
think clearly. A person with low blood sugar rarely feels like talking
and may become irritated if you try to start a conversation. Instead
of talking, try bringing something that will help the attack (such as a
cup of fruit juice) and set it down by the person. If the person is
having a low blood sugar, he will probably drink the juice. If he
doesn't, you might ask if he's feeling all right. If his response is
normal, tell him you think his blood sugar is low and ask him to test
it. If you get a response that's not so normal (such as an angry stare,
or "Why are you bothering me!"), this may be a sign that the person
needs help. Ask him to please drink the juice. If he is very confused,
you might try to use glucagon. Glucagon is a hormone injection that
raises blood sugar levels quickly. It is recommended that everyone
who uses insulin have a glucagon kit on hand for emergencies. If
the person you're trying to help is well prepared, they will probably
have some available.

*W*hy do I feel shaky, sweaty, and have a
pounding heart when my blood sugar is
normal?

▼
TIP:

You could be having a panic attack. The symptoms of a panic
attack include feelings of terror, shakiness, sweatiness, and a
pounding heart. As you probably know, these are the symptoms
caused by low blood sugar. Often it is your fear of something happening that actually triggers a panic attack. If you're worried about
what might happen if "this or that" occurs, you can trigger your
adrenalin, and it's the adrenalin that causes the symptoms. The
symptoms cause your fear to further increase and you feel out of
control. For example, just the fear of having a low blood sugar reac-
tion might be enough to trigger this vicious cycle. Also keep in
mind that if your blood sugar is usually very high, and then quickly
drops to normal levels, you can experience these symptoms.

If you think you are having panic attacks, counseling may be
helpful. If the fears that are triggering the attacks are related to your
diabetes, a few sessions of diabetes counseling should help you feel
more in control. Also, some medications have been shown to reduce
the intensity and frequency of anxiety attacks. Ask your diabetes
care team for more information.

Chapter 2
MEDICATIONS AND YOU

*B*esides keeping my cholesterol level low, is there anything I can do to prevent heart disease?

▼
TIP:

Heart disease is the number one killer of people with diabetes. Many of the strategies for preventing heart disease are well known: stop smoking, control your blood pressure (less then 130/80), keep your LDL cholesterol level below 100, exercise regularly, and eat healthy. Other strategies, however, are less well publicized, are still being studied, or are too specific to people with diabetes to receive much media attention. For example, a recent study of drugs called ACE inhibitors has shown that the risk of having a heart attack or dying from cardiovascular disease was reduced by 25% to 30% among people with diabetes who took an ACE inhibitor. This was true even if the people did not have high blood pressure or a history of heart disease. Since ACE inhibitors have been shown to help people with diabetes by reducing the progression of kidney disease, many physicians are prescribing ACE inhibitors to reduce heart disease in their patients.

Taking a low dose aspirin (81 mg) daily may also reduce the risk of heart disease. To avoid stomach problems, use enteric-coated aspirin.

*I*s there an upper limit to how much insulin I
can take for my diabetes?

TIP:

There is no upper limit to the insulin dose you can take. Most
people with diabetes need between 1/2 and 1 unit of insulin per
kilogram of body weight per day to control their diabetes. That means
35–70 units per day for an average 150-pound person. Needing any
more than this is usually a sign of insulin resistance. Some very
insulin-resistant people can require hundreds of units of insulin per
day to control their blood sugars. A few medical scientists have
argued that patients with type 2 diabetes and insulin resistance should
be treated with insulin sensitizing agents rather than insulin. They
think that high levels of insulin increase the risk for cardiovascular
disease, though there is no strong evidence to support this.

A principal side effect of using high doses of insulin is a 5% to
15% weight gain. The most important thing to keep in mind is that
high blood glucose is more dangerous than an increase in medication, so talk to your doctor and do whatever it takes to get your
blood glucose down.

*C*an I take my insulin without using a
needle?

▼

TIP:

Many people prefer to inject insulin with an insulin injector. Insulin injectors have become smaller and more convenient and no longer require a prescription. They work by using compressed air to inject the insulin. You dial up the dose of insulin you want, press a button, and inject the insulin into your skin. Some individuals find that this is less painful than needle sticks. If you have a child with diabetes or a phobia of needles, insulin injectors can be an attractive choice. In addition, some studies show that insulin is absorbed more rapidly with injectors, since the insulin is more evenly dispersed than with needles.

The downside of insulin injectors is how expensive they are. Compared to needles, they're pretty pricey. You can obtain more information about insulin injectors by visiting a company's website, such as that available from the Medi-Ject Corporation for the Medi-Jector, at *www.mediject.com*, or you can call toll-free at 1-800-328-3074. They will send you a free video describing the Medi-Jector. Other available jet injectors include Advanta Jet (Activa Brand Products, Inc.), Gentle Jet (Activa Brand Products, Inc.), Advanta Jet ES (Activa Brand Products, Inc.), Vitajet 3 (Bioject Corp.), Injex (Equidyne Corp.), and At Last (Amira).

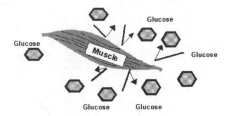

What is insulin resistance?

▼
TIP:

Resistance to insulin is a trait of type 2 diabetes. However, people without diabetes and people with type 1 diabetes can also have insulin resistance.

Basically, insulin resistance keeps your liver, muscles, and fat cells from working as they should. When working properly, insulin signals your liver that you have eaten and that it should store the extra glucose as starch. In between meals your liver makes glucose to supply the brain with energy. If you have insulin resistance, you're unable to stop the liver from making glucose, so your liver keeps making glucose even when you don't need it. In muscles, insulin allows cells to absorb glucose so that it can be used for muscle energy. If you have insulin resistance, muscles do not transport glucose into the cells well. In fat cells, insulin causes you to grow and store fat for use when you don't eat. This process is sluggish if you have insulin resistance.

To make up for insulin resistance in your liver and muscle cells, your pancreas produces too much insulin. After awhile, your body won't be able to keep up with this demand, your insulin levels drop, blood sugar levels get higher, and, eventually, you have diabetes.

*W*ill insulin analogs improve my diabetes
treatment plan?

▼
TIP:

An insulin analog is a form of human insulin that is slightly
different from the insulin that is secreted from the human
pancreas. Surprisingly, these insulin analogs may work better than
the insulin your body would normally produce. When your pancreas
releases insulin, it secretes it into your bloodstream. When used to
treat diabetes, insulin is usually injected under your skin, not into the
bloodstream. Unfortunately, injected insulin may not be absorbed fast
enough to be really effective. Insulin analogues are designed to help
this process. By altering the chemical structure of human insulin, it
can be more quickly absorbed, making it more effective when you eat
a meal.

There are two choices of rapid-acting insulin analogs—insulin
lispro and insulin aspart. Both insulin analogs are safe and can be
injected 0–15 minutes before a meal. In addition, a long-acting
insulin analog, insulin glargine ("glar-jeen"), is now available. It
provides a steady level of background insulin throughout the day
and night after one injection. This insulin does not have to be
agitated before you inject it, but because of its acidity, it cannot be
mixed with short-acting insulins.

A re there any new insulins that could simplify my diabetes care?

▼
TIP:

Yes. It's called insulin glargine. This man-made insulin is very similar to human insulin but it's designed to be more slowly absorbed from your skin. This means it only needs to be taken once a day. It gives you a very stable, effective background insulin level upon which you can add rapid-acting insulin for each meal (if you have type 1 diabetes) or no other insulin at all (if you have well-controlled type 2 diabetes). Several large clinical studies using insulin glargine have shown that it is better than NPH and ultralente insulin at providing a steady-state level of insulin in your blood.

If you are currently taking a combination of a long-acting and a rapid-acting insulin, you can substitute insulin glargine for your long-acting insulin. However, you can't combine insulin glargine with rapid-acting insulins in the syringe, so separate injections are necessary.

*C*an I premix my insulin lispro (Humalog)
with NPH insulin and keep the syringe in
my purse until lunch?

▼
TIP:

You're probably aware that you can mix short-acting insulins or
regular insulin with NPH insulin and inject them immediately
without any problem. However, some worry that if these insulins are
mixed and then kept for several hours, the NPH insulin will change
some of the regular insulin to a longer-acting form of insulin. In fact,
the package insert for insulin lispro suggests that you should not prefill the syringe with both insulins without injecting them immediately.
However, a recent study has shown that these mixed insulins are
stable for up to 28 days and can be taken without any major
problems, with one exception. If you usually mix the two insulins,
and then decide not to prefill one day (or vice versa), the short acting
insulin (insulin lispro) will act differently.

Therefore, yes, you can mix the two insulins and keep them in
your purse until you need them, but only if you plan on doing this
every day. Be sure to mix the insulins (except with ultralente
insulin). Importantly, Humalog should not be mixed with ultralente
insulin more than 5 minutes prior to injection because ultralente will
delay the onset of activity in the Humalog.

*S*hould I be afraid to start taking insulin?

TIP:

If you've been asked to start taking insulin, you may have some initial fears. You may believe that your diabetes is not "serious" as long as you don't have to take insulin. Or you may believe that being on insulin means you have failed in your diabetes management. Or you might have a fear of needles. But you doctor has good reasons for wanting you to start insulin, some of which may include:

- Your body is no longer responding effectively to oral medication.
- Insulin may be more affordable.
- You do not like the side effects of oral medication.
- Oral medications are not safe for you. For example, if you are on dialysis, oral medications can be dangerous.

Insulin is one of the most powerful medications we have to keep blood sugars down. Nowadays, there are ways to take insulin that are very flexible, including needle-free solutions to injecting. Talk to your diabetes team and with other people who take insulin to find out the regimen that will work best for you. You will find that instead of making things more complicated and serious, taking insulin may make your life with diabetes easier.

*W*here can I get more information on
insulin sensitizers?

▼
TIP:

Insulin sensitizers are the newest oral medications approved for type
2 diabetes. They can be effectively used with other medications and
have allowed many individuals to stop insulin injections and use only
oral medications. The first medication on the market was troglitazone
(Rezulin), which was extremely popular in Japan and the United
States. Unfortunately, it was very toxic to the liver and has been taken
off the market. Currently, there are two FDA-approved insulin
sensitizers on the market—rosiglitazone (Avandia) and pioglitazone
(Actose). Neither of these have shown serious danger to the liver in
animals or humans. You should be aware that these medications
might cause you to retain fluids, which may require you to take a
diuretic (water pill). Metformin also increases sensitivity to insulin
but is not usually thought of as an "insulin sensitizer." Its primary
function is to decrease your liver's ability to make sugar.

Information on each of these medications may be obtained from
the company's website. The website for Avandia is
www.avandia.com, or you can call 1-800-282-6342. For Actose, the
website address is *www.actose.com*, or you can call 1-877-825-3327.
Ask your doctor or diabetes care team if you have any questions.

*C**an I take a pill to lose weight?*

▼
TIP:

One new drug called orlistat (Xenical) has been tested in people with type 2 diabetes and can probably be used safely. This drug works by not allowing your body to absorb fats from the food you eat. As a result, dietary fats are not digested. In a study of 391 seriously overweight men with type 2 diabetes, men taking orlistat lost about 6% of their body weight, on average, over a one-year period compared to about a 4% weight loss in men taking a placebo (a "dummy pill"). This is a 4-pound difference in a 200-pound man ($200 \times 6\% = 12$ pounds; $200 \times 4\% = 8$ pounds). Blood sugars went down in both groups and were only slightly lower in the orlistat group. Because the drug doesn't allow you to absorb as much fat, you might be at risk for low levels of fat soluble vitamins, such as vitamin A, E, K, and D. If you're taking orlistat, you should consider taking a vitamin supplement. While orlistat can aid in weight loss, it's no replacement for healthy eating and an exercise strategy. Weigh the costs and the benefits and speak with your diabetes care team before deciding whether or not orlistat is the right approach for you.

Chapter 3
PLANNING YOUR MEALS

If I eat the right foods, does the amount matter?

TIP:

Whether you're eating ice cream or carrot sticks, portion size does matter. Body weight increases, decreases, or stays the same based on how many calories you eat versus how many calories you burn. If the calories you eat equal the calories you use, your weight will remain the same. On the other hand, if you burn more calories than you take in, you can expect to lose weight. It is important to eat a variety of healthy foods, and even more important to eat the recommended portions. Eating too much of one type of food, or not enough of another, can be unhealthy. When the urge to eat is too strong, try eating "free foods." Free foods are items that have less than 20 calories per serving. All items must be sugar-free and should be low fat. Below is a list of some free foods.

Drinks—bouillon, diet sodas, diet club soda, diet tonic water

Fruits—1/2 cup cranberries, 1/2 cup rhubarb

Vegetables/Greens—cabbage, celery, cucumber, green onion, mushrooms, radishes, zucchini, endive, escarole, lettuce, romaine, spinach

Sweet Substitutes—sugar-free candy, gelatin, sugar-free gum, sugar-free jam, sugar-free jelly

Condiments—mustard, taco sauce, vinegar

Does fast food like pizza fit into my meal plan?

▼
TIP:

Diabetes meal plans have changed quite a bit in the last decade. In the past, people with type 1 diabetes were told to follow rigid eating patterns. Rich foods like pizza and ice cream were strictly off limits. The timing, amount, and kind of food you ate were restricted, and the food you ate had to be matched to your insulin dose. Luckily, things are a little more flexible now. Since the availability of rapid-acting insulin (such as insulin lispro), people with type 1 diabetes can follow a normal, balanced diet. Insulin can be matched to your daily lifestyle, instead of the other way around. For example, a salad with chicken strips and a diet cola might require one or two units of insulin. Two slices of pizza, a glass of milk, and ice cream might require 10 units. With training from your diabetes care team and a little personal experience, you can learn how much insulin you need to control your blood sugars for different types of meals. If you are using the old style therapy of pattern control, talk to your diabetes care team about how to change your therapy to the food you eat. You may also contact the American Association of Diabetes Educators at (800) 832-6874 to find someone who can help you with your diabetes meal plans.

*W**hy do I eat more than I should in the evenings?*

▼
TIP:

M any people eat sensibly during the day, only to eat too much at night. This can make it hard to keep blood sugars under control. There could be several reasons why you eat too much or eat the wrong foods at night. Maybe you've been trying so hard to eat "healthy" that you are feeling deprived of some of your "comfort" foods. Perhaps you manage to ignore uncomfortable feelings like depression, anxiety, loneliness, or even boredom during the day, but these feelings surface once the sun goes down. If these reasons explain why you are eating more at night, you have taken the first step toward changing that pattern. The following is an example of small steps you might take to change your pattern:

- **Step 1**—Figure out why you overeat in the evenings. For example, you're strict with your diet during the day and you miss the cookies you usually eat for lunch.
- **Step 2**—Figure out what might be a healthier response. Have a plan for cookie cravings in the evening. Try eating one with lunch and three at night, instead of four all at once. Then, slowly decrease the amount you eat over time.
- **Step 3**—Substitute a healthier snack, such as a fruit, for the cookie.

*H*ow can I eat less fat at a fast food
restaurant?

▼
TIP:

Since most fast food restaurants have adopted the "bigger is better"
attitude, classic small, medium, and large sizes are no longer
available. Now you have large, extra large, and supersize. Because of
these larger portion sizes, the average American takes in 150 more
calories a day, and most of these calories are fat. Although an extra
150 calories a day doesn't sound like much, these calories add up
with bad results for you. There are many ways you can lower calories
and fat in a fast food restaurant. The easiest way is to choose the
smallest serving available. Just choosing a plain cheeseburger instead
of a double cheeseburger will remove more than 200 calories. Most
important is to choose low-fat items in place of high-fat items. For
example, choose a baked potato with salsa or steak sauce (instead of
butter and sour cream) to replace French fries. Order sandwiches
without fancy sauces, and order salads with low-fat dressings (or "on-
the-side" to control the amount of dressing you put on your salad).
When low-fat options are not available, leave a few fries on your
plate or a few bites of your sandwich, and skip dessert. The best way
to reduce fat in fast food? Reduce how often you eat fast food.

*W*ill *the new high-protein, low-carbohydrate diets help me lose weight?*

▼

TIP:

Popular low-carbohydrate diets promise quick weight loss while you take in unlimited calories from protein and fat. People who support these diets claim that carbohydrates are harmful because they increase the insulin levels in your blood. They suggest high insulin levels cause obesity, which leads to many other problems, including diabetes. All of this sounds exciting. Finally, a "magic" way to lose weight. Unfortunately, it's not that simple. Severely reducing carbohydrates in your diet can give you quick weight loss, but there may be consequences. The quick weight you lose from these diets is mostly water loss. Carbohydrates are the main fuel for many of your body's systems (including the brain). If there is not enough carbohydrate coming in, your body turns to different energy sources. Your body first uses stored glucose (glycogen) and when that runs out, the protein in your muscles may be converted to sugar. Fat is also broken down for energy. This sounds good, but the breakdown can give you nausea, constipation, and low energy. If you have diabetes, you may be at a higher risk for some of the more severe consequences of a low-carbohydrate diet, such as diabetic ketoacidosis. The best way to lose weight, and keep it off, is still the "calories in" vs. "calories out" method. At this time there are no long-term scientific studies to support the claims of low-carbohydrate diets.

*H*ow can I keep from gaining weight
during the holidays?

▼ TIP:

T he reasons for weight gain (and high blood sugars!) during the
holiday season are no mystery. People gain weight during the
holidays because they eat too much and get less physical activity.
This does not have to happen. The holiday season is a time for
renewing family and spiritual ties through tradition. If you have
diabetes, a healthy response to the holiday season may include
beginning new traditions. For example, substituting pumpkin custard
for pumpkin pie as the traditional dessert for Thanksgiving dinner
will get rid of the piecrust (and a lot of calories). Most importantly,
you should maintain your daily routine as much as possible. That
means getting out of bed at your usual time, testing your blood sugar
at regular intervals, eating only at mealtime, and performing your
daily exercise. If you take care of yourself during the holidays, you
will feel better and reduce the chance for unwanted weight gain.

*W*hat are the advantages of a low-fat meal plan?

TIP:

S taying on a diet is difficult. Cutting down on the food you eat can result in a cycle of weight loss followed by weight gain. Fat has more than twice as many calories per gram as either protein or carbohydrate. If you cut fat, you will cut calories. A low-fat meal plan helps you:

- lose weight
- lower cholesterol
- improve your blood lipids
- lower your risk for cardiovascular disease
- reduce your risk for colon cancer, since a low-fat meal plan is associated with high fiber
- eat larger portions of food without the calories
- improve your self-esteem

So do what you can to cut fat from your eating and you'll be well on your way to better health.

*H*ow can I organize my meal
preparation?

▼
TIP:

I't's hard to find the time to do anything anymore. Still, sticking with your meal plan is important. By planning time for food chores and cooking you can save time later. The following schedule allows you to stick to your meal plan while cooking only once a month.

1. Sit down with your family and make a list of their favorite foods (1/2 hour).
2. From that list, put together menus for six days (1/2 hour).
3. Make a shopping list of the food and supplies needed to make these meals and multiply the list by four. Remember to include freezer bags (1/2 hour).
4. Shop for all the food and supplies (2.5 hours).
5. Take one whole day or two evenings and cook four meals worth of all the dishes you have chosen. Freeze everything in portion sizes big enough for one meal. (6–8 hours).
6. Go out to dinner and relax.
7. You now have 24 days of meals prepared. Rotate menus each day for the next four weeks. The remaining days of the month are for eating out (remember, you still need to eat healthy).

Using this plan, it will take you about 12 hours to prepare a month's worth of meals.

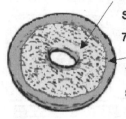

Sauce & Cheese
70 calories

½ Bagel
80 calories

Is it okay for me to eat snacks?

▼
TIP:

Absolutely! In fact, snacks can be a very important part of your meal plan. Many people think of snacks as the same as "junk food." This is not always the case. Snacking can be healthy and can help you avoid being hungry all the time. It can be designed to fit your needs and your diabetes management plan. However, snacks *must* be included in your total meal plan. Don't overdo snacks just like you don't overdo eating your regular foods. One way to do this is to schedule your snacks. It is often helpful to have your snacks at the same time each day. What time of day do you get hungry—mid-morning, mid-afternoon, evening, all the time? Choosing healthy snacks may get you through the day without overeating. Healthy snacks do not have to be "fat free" either. If not eaten too much, fat is an important source of energy. Talk with your diabetes care team to help you plan for a tasty snack like a bagel pizza. The *Snack, Munch, Nibble Nosh Book* is available through the American Diabetes Association bookstore and has many healthy snack recipes.

*W*hat foods should I keep on hand for quick *meal preparation and snacks?*

▼
TIP:

T his depends on a lot of things. Every person has different tastes and preferences. However, some foods are good to keep available for last-minute meals or healthy snacks no matter what your taste preference. These foods can be combined to make many different items. They are healthy, low fat, and will not spoil quickly. Be sure to check labels and don't eat out-dated foods. Below are some foods that you may want to keep on hand.

vegetables (mixed and varieties)

fruits (water packed)

meats (water packed, low fat, low salt)

soups/broth (low fat, low sodium)

evaporated milk

tomato sauces (low fat)

macaroni

spaghetti

beans

rice

peanut butter (low fat)

pudding (low fat, low sugar)

gelatin (low sugar)

spices/Worcester-shire sauce

cooking spray oil

salad dressing (low fat)

mustard/mayon-naise (low fat)

salsa/relish

fruit spread (low sugar)

syrup (low sugar)

soda crackers

graham crackers

flour/biscuit mix/ pancake mix

non-fat dry milk powder

spices

*C*an people with diabetes eat foods
that contain sugar?

▼
TIP:

In the past, sugar was strictly off limits for people who had
diabetes. It was believed that simple sugar (like table sugar) would
be more quickly absorbed and lead to a higher blood sugar than other
carbohydrates. Research has shown that this is not true. The
American Diabetes Association has relaxed its guidelines on sugar for
people with diabetes. Now you can eat foods containing sugar. Just be
sure to count the sugars as part of your total carbohydrates, just as
you would with starches. Many exchange lists exclude dessert foods.
Below is a chart giving approximate carbohydrate counts for some
sample dessert foods:

Dessert	Size: 1 exchange, which is 15 grams of carbohydrate or 1 bread or fruit exchange
Cake, unfrosted	1 1/2 in square
Cake, with frosting	1 inch square
Ice cream, ice milk, sherbet, frozen yogurt	1/2 cup
Cookies, round sandwich type	1 cookie
Table sugar	1 tablespoon

*H*ow do I get protein in my diet if I am
vegetarian?

▼
TIP:

Many foods contain protein, but meat, eggs, and dairy foods contain "complete proteins." Grains and legumes (beans, peas, and lentils) contain "incomplete proteins." If your vegetarian diet includes eggs and/or dairy products, then your diet likely provides enough "complete proteins." If you do not eat eggs or dairy foods you must combine two incomplete protein foods in a meal so that each meal provides the complete proteins you need.

The following table shows some of the ways incomplete proteins can be combined to make a complete protein:

Rice plus:	Wheat plus:	Legumes plus:
Wheat	Legumes	Corn
or	or	or
legumes	soybeans and nuts	rice
or	or	or
sesame seeds	soybeans and rice	wheat

The serving size is 1/3–1/2 cup.

Your diabetes care team and a dietitian can determine your protein needs, as well as your likes and dislikes, to create a meal plan that works for you.

*I*s white cheese better for my diabetic diet than yellow cheese?

TIP:

N o. All cheeses (hard, soft, and processed) have a high fat content. Color is added to cheese and is not related to how much fat is in the cheese. In most cheeses, about 75% of the calories come from fat! There are several "low-fat" cheeses on the market, but the taste and texture are usually different from regular cheese. Read the labels and experiment with different varieties to find the types you enjoy most. The chart below lists cheeses, the percent fat for a 1-ounce serving (about one slice), and exchange information for each cheese. More "cheesy" information can be found using the Internet. The key words to use are "cheese" or "diet and nutrition."

Cheese (1 ounce)	% fat	Diabetic exchanges
Cheddar	74	1 meat
Mozzarella	56	1 medium fat
Bleu	73	1 medium fat
Feta	59	1/2 medium fat
Parmesan	62	2 medium fats
Velveeta®	62	1 medium fat
Brie	75	2 fats
Swiss	66	1/2 fat plus 1 medium meat
Gouda	69	1/2 fat plus 1 medium meat
Cream Cheese	90	2 fats

*D*o I need to pay attention to how much fiber I eat?

▼
TIP:

Fiber is the part of plant food that doesn't get digested. The ADA recommends eating 20 to 35 grams of fiber each day. Fiber is important in your diet because it can slow the absorption of sugar into your blood. Fiber helps your bowels stay regular, lowers the level of cholesterol in your blood, and helps you feel full and satisfied. Some studies have also shown high-fiber diets can improve HbA1c. Fiber is found in whole grains, breads, rice, pasta, dried beans and legumes, as well as fruits and vegetables. These foods may also reduce your risk for colon cancer and heart disease. If you eat a diet rich in these foods, you will not need a fiber supplement.

Food	Portion size	Fiber	Exchange rate
Rolled oat meal	1/2 cup dry	4 grams	2 bread exchanges
Whole wheat bread	1 oz slice	2 grams	1 bread exchange
Green peas	2/3 cup	4 grams	1 bread exchange
Wax beans	2/3 cup	2 grams fiber	Not counted as an exchange
Apple	1 large	5 grams fiber	2 fruit exchanges

Chapter 4
GET MOVING!

*H*ow do I know if my exercise program is "aerobic"?

▼
TIP:

The term "aerobic" refers to exercise that increases your heart rate. You can check your heart rate (or pulse rate) with the help of a stopwatch or a watch with a second hand. Place your index and middle finger on your wrist, just below the base of your thumb, or on your neck on either side of your Adam's apple. Count the number of beats for 15 seconds and then multiply this number by 4 to determine your heart rate per minute. Your resting heart rate should be 60–100 beats per minute. To find if your exercise program is aerobic, determine your target heart rate range (see chart below) and count your heart rate during or after exercise. When any activity raises your heart rate to within your target heart rate range, you are "aerobic."

Age	Normal resting heart rate	Target heart rate range
30–39 yrs	60–100	95–133
40–49 yrs	60–100	90–126
50–59 yrs	60–100	85–119
60–69 yrs	60–100	80–112
70–79 yrs	60–100	75–105
80–89 yrs	60–100	70–98
90+ yrs	60–100	65–91

*C*an I consider household chores
  exercise?

▼
TIP:

Yes. Have you ever raced around the house to get the dusting and
vacuuming done before guests arrive, and then found you're out
of energy? Have you noticed your blood glucose level gets low
whenever you mow the lawn? The U.S. Surgeon General suggests
30 minutes of moderate physical activity at least 5 days per week.
Moderate intensity is anything that raises your heart rate. Thirty
minutes sounds like a lot, but you don't have to do it all at once. If
your chores increase your heart rate for 10 minutes or more, you can
count it toward your exercise goal. Ten straight minutes of moderate
intensity activity 3 times per day would give you the recommended
30-minute workout. Mowing your lawn with a push mower, moving
furniture when you vacuum, chopping wood, and washing the floor
on your hands and knees are all good examples of moderate intensity
exercise. Light dusting, washing dishes, and ironing are considered to
be light intensity activities and would not count toward your daily
activity minutes. So, go ahead . . . retire the housekeeper and the lawn
crew—do these household chores yourself and build a healthier you!

*W**hy should I exercise?*

▼
TIP:

B ecause it might save your life! Exercise has been recommended for people with diabetes for many years and is one of the basic elements of diabetes treatment. However, it was not scientifically proven that exercise led to better health or a longer life span with diabetes until recently. In a new study, more than 1200 men with type 2 diabetes were followed for an average period of 12 years. Death rates in these men were examined based on their level of physical fitness. Men who said that they were not physically active had a 70% higher death rate compared to men who were. In addition, men in the lowest fitness group had double the death rate of the men in the highest fitness group. Exercise continued to help even after other factors—such as glucose levels, cholesterol levels, body weight, smoking, and high blood pressure—were under control. So now we can say with certainty that exercise can help you live a longer, healthier life with type 2 diabetes. This is the best reason we can give you to get off the couch and start exercising!

*D*oes my diabetes make it harder for me to exercise?

TIP:

It's possible that if you are not in good shape, having diabetes might make exercise harder for you, especially at first. Researchers believe there is a possibility that diabetes may damage the cells that line the blood vessels, which would mean your blood vessels wouldn't dilate correctly during exercise. To get blood to your muscles while you exercise, your blood vessels need to dilate normally. If this doesn't happen, it may be harder for you to do the same exercise as another person your age or in the same shape as you. This can be frustrating, and may make it difficult for you to keep exercising. Even though it is hard, it's worth it to make the effort. Research has shown that exercise lowers blood sugar and cuts down on stress. Keep in mind that exercise will affect your blood sugar levels. If you're just starting out, you may need to adjust your medication to match these blood sugar changes. Remember— exercise gets easier the more you do it. Once you get in the swing of things, diabetes should not keep you from meeting your exercise goals.

How can I measure the distance I walk each day?

▼
TIP:

A pedometer is a little, watch-sized device that counts your steps for you. Pedometers can be found at most sporting goods stores and cost about $15.00. Pedometers need to be attached to your clothing around your waist first thing in the morning and worn the entire day. Begin the first few days recording your steps and log this number on your calendar. If you walk fewer than 8000–10,000 steps per day, you need to increase your daily activity. Fewer than 8,000 steps per day is considered sedentary, which means you're not getting enough exercise. Between 8,000 and 10,000 steps is considered active. Increase your total daily steps by walking 100 extra steps every day. Set a higher goal each month until you are walking 9000–10,000 steps per day. Then try to build up to more than 10,000 steps each day. Depending upon the length of your stride, these additional steps will add up to approximately 2 miles. This can help you lose weight and feel better. So keep walking!

*D*o I need a personal trainer to help me with
my exercise program?

TIP:

Apersonal trainer is not necessary. However, if you no longer see
results from your exercise, can't reach your weight goal, or are
just bored with your routine, a personal trainer can help you get back
on track. Just two or three sessions with a personal trainer can be
helpful. Most gyms offer personal trainers free of charge if you're a
member. When choosing a trainer, be careful. Many people who
claim to be trainers are not professionally certified. It is important
that you know how to choose a certified personal trainer. Listed
below are three organizations that certify trainers.

- American College of Sports Medicine (ACSM)
- American College of Exercise (ACE)
- National Strength and Conditioning Association (NSCA)

If your trainer is certified by any of these organizations you can be
sure that he or she is a professional. For more information, you may
contact your gym manager or use the website *www.acefitness.org*
for help.

Chapter 5
WHAT TO DO WITH
HEALTH CARE

*H*ow can I make the most out of my appointments with my diabetes care team?

▼
TIP:

There are several ways you can get the most from your appointment. For instance:

- Be prepared and come a little early to allow time for check-in.
- If you were told to get lab tests, get them done several days before your appointment. If they were done somewhere else, call to make sure your results were sent to your doctor's office. It might be up to you to get the results and bring them with you to the visit.
- Bring your blood sugar meter and a log of your blood sugar readings. If you do not check your blood sugars regularly, take several blood glucose readings before meals and two hours after meals during the week before your appointment.
- Bring your prescription bottles with you. If you are taking vitamins, supplements, or herbal remedies, bring them with you, too.
- Jot down questions you want to ask your diabetes care team.
- If you need a referral, make sure you have it with you when you go to your appointment.
- Bring a pen and paper to write down instructions and other information.
- Take off your shoes and socks as soon as you get into the room so that your provider can examine your feet.

*W*hat should I do if my diabetes treatment plan
isn't working?

▼

TIP:

*I*f you are not meeting your diabetes treatment goals, one of two
things could be happening:

1. You are not completely following your treatment plan.
2. Your treatment plan is not right for you.

Meet with a Certified Diabetes Educator or a Registered Dietitian to
talk about your diet if you have not yet done so or if it has been
longer than two years since you've had any dietary counseling. You
may also need to meet with an exercise trainer if there's something
keeping you from regular exercise. An exercise trainer can design an
exercise plan that fits your abilities. Finally, discuss your medications with your doctor. Are you taking them in the right amount and
at the right time of day? The American Diabetes Association states
that an HbA1c level of less than 7.0% is what you're shooting for
with therapy. If your doctor's care does not give you an HbA1c of
less than 8.0%, it's time to talk with your diabetes care team. You
can request a meeting with a diabetologist or a Certified Diabetes
Educator. He or she will work with your diabetes care team to help
you meet the goals of your diabetes treatment plan.

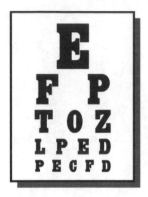

*H*ow often should I get my eyes examined?

▼
TIP:

Currently, the American Diabetes Association recommends that if you have diabetes you should have your eyes checked by an ophthalmologist once a year. However, this is not a rigid recommendation. Doctors have suggested that in some patients, an eye exam every two to three years is enough. You probably do not need an eye exam every year if:

■ you have had a recent normal eye exam
■ you have had type 1 diabetes for less than 10 years
■ you have excellent glucose control
■ you do not also have diseases that lead to a high rate of retinopathy, such as high blood pressure or kidney disease.

If you have background retinopathy (changes in the back of your eye that indicate your diabetes is affecting your eye but not threatening your vision at the moment) you should continue to have yearly eye exams. The best person to recommend how often you should get an eye exam is your own eye doctor. Be sure to ask him at your next visit how often you should get an eye exam.

*H*ow *can my social security check*
cover the cost of a healthy meal
plan?

▼
TIP:

W hen your personal income only covers the bare essentials, it's difficult to afford healthy foods like cherries, bell peppers, and whole wheat bread. If you want to make healthier food choices, how can you fit it into your budget? Your community may be the answer. The government and your community offer many programs to help people eat healthy. These programs are not charity. They're a public service to the entire community. Look through the city and government pages of your telephone book for the following:

- Health Department
- Families First Program
- Women, Infant, and Children Program
- Human Services Department
- Senior Services
- Senior Companion Program
- Family and Community Services

These resources can help you get the healthy meals you need. And remember, unhealthy food such as fast food and processed food can be even more expensive than healthy food. Try to get the food your body needs. It's worth the effort.

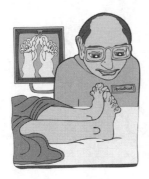

*H*ow can I keep my feet healthy?

▼
TIP:

First of all, it's good that you're concerned about your feet. People with diabetes often develop foot problems, but some simple care can prevent complications. Try the following.

- Keep your feet clean and don't forget to check them every day. Better yet, have someone check your feet for you.
- Make sure someone trims your nails on a regular schedule.
- If you have toenail problems, poor circulation, and/or nerve damage, you should see a podiatrist.
- Be sure to wear socks or shoe inserts that absorb sweat.
- Always check your shoes for foreign objects.
- Make sure that new shoes fit properly and take the time to break them in slowly.
- When you find shoes that are particularly comfortable, buy two pairs.
- Try wearing two different pairs of shoes every day. Wear one pair to work in the morning, and then change into the other pair half way through the day. If you alternate shoes each day, it's better for your feet and for your shoes.

For additional tips on foot care, see another book in this series, *101 Foot Care Tips for People with Diabetes.*

H *ow can I get my HMO to provide*
better care for my diabetes?

▼
TIP:

G etting proper medical care can be tricky with managed health
care, but you'll probably find that you can get excellent care
once you have learned how to work the system. Your primary care
provider is the key to getting good care in a Health Maintenance
Organization (HMO). He or she is the person who can help you find
resources in your health care organization, including specialists,
diabetes educators, and dietitians. You must also know the current
standards of care for diabetes. Make it clear to your primary care
provider that you expect these standards to be met. This means
providing the supplies you need for home blood glucose monitoring,
testing of your HbA1c level every three months, prescribing
medications, and yearly checkups of your eyes, kidneys, and
cholesterol levels. Finally, many HMO's have special programs for
people with chronic diseases like diabetes. Ask your primary care
provider about Case Management services in your HMO. Case
managers include nurses, social workers, and diabetes educators.
Case managers can be helpful because they know the ropes and can
help you get through the red tape of your HMO.

*W*hat vaccinations should I receive if I have diabetes?

TIP:

Vaccinations are very important for everyone, but even more so if you have diabetes. This is because high blood sugar may lower your body's ability to fight infections. Below is a list of the vaccinations you should get if you have diabetes.

- Flu (influenza)—Including pregnant women who are in their second or third trimester during the flu season.
- Pneumonia—Especially if you've had your spleen removed.
- Hepatitis A—Especially if you're traveling to a foreign country that may not have clean water and good sewage disposal. Also, if you have liver or kidney disease or blood clotting disorders.
- Hepatitis B—Especially health care workers, travelers to certain countries, people on dialysis, and people who must receive donor blood products.
- Measles, mumps, rubella—If you were born in 1957 or later.
- Chicken pox—If you are 13 years or older and have not already had chicken pox.

Vaccinations may not be safe for everyone, so be sure and talk to your diabetes care team about which vaccinations are right for you.

*H*ow can I throw away my insulin syringes safely?

▼
TIP:

W hile it's true that insulin syringes in your trash can be a health risk to the people who handle your trash, there are no laws that require you to throw away your used syringes any special way. On the other hand, hospitals and medical clinics are required to dispose of sharp medical waste in puncture-resistant containers. The companies that make insulin syringes also make containers that allow you to dispose of syringes safely. However, these containers are often expensive and hard to find. If you use insulin syringes, you can safely throw them away by putting them in a strong plastic container with a lid, such as a used milk bottle or an empty dishwashing or laundry detergent bottle. Make sure the lid is tight and won't come off. People with blood-borne diseases such as hepatitis or HIV should be very careful of how they get rid of their insulin syringes and should discuss what they can do to be safe with their diabetes care team.

*W*ill my mother receive good care for her
diabetes in a nursing home?

▼ TIP:

It's possible, but not certain. Diabetes is common among the elderly. Unfortunately, since some patients in nursing homes suffer from other serious and chronic conditions, day-to-day diabetes care may be overlooked. It is important to find out if your mother's nursing home follows the ADA guidelines for standard care. You or another family member may want to meet with the nursing home staff and see how they handle diabetes. Questions you might ask:

- How many times a day is blood sugar monitored?
- When are diabetes medicines given during the day?
- What are the diabetes treatment goals?
- How often will her feet be checked?
- How quickly is hypoglycemia recognized and treated?
- Is blood pressure normally monitored?

You should also see if they evaluate for diabetic complications of the eye, kidney, and heart at least once a year. Schedule a periodic review of her status with the charge nurse or administrator. By making it clear that you expect excellent diabetes care for your mother, you can help make your mother's stay at the nursing home a positive experience.

*W*hat is involved in starting insulin pump
therapy?

▼
TIP:

S tarting pump therapy takes time and money. However, most insulin plans will cover insulin pumps (which cost about $5,000) for patients with type 1 diabetes. Supplies (tubing, insulin reservoir, adhesive tape, iv prep, etc.) add another $100 to $200 a month. It then takes several hours of training to learn to use a pump. This training includes:

- Checking your blood glucose after food, activity, and medicine.
- Reviewing the factors that are affecting your highs and lows.
- Adjusting the doses to find what works for you.
- Reviewing your meal plan strategy with a registered dietitian.
- More structure in your daily routine until your insulin needs have been determined.

Once your training period is complete, you will probably have better diabetes control and fewer episodes of low blood sugar. Ask your diabetes care team to refer you to someone who uses a pump and is willing to discuss his or her experiences. It is important to take the time to learn about insulin pumps before making a decision to buy one.

Should I refrigerate my insulin?

▼
TIP:

The vials of insulin that you are using right now should be left at room temperature and away from heat sources and light. Don't leave insulin in your car where it can become hot or cold very quickly. If you take insulin with your food, you need to keep that insulin with you. You probably don't need to carry an insulin cooler. Your pocket or purse will work just fine (just don't leave it some place that's very warm or cold), since modern insulin is stable for at least one month at room temperature.

You should keep unopened vials of insulin in the refrigerator but never in the freezer. However, don't put the vials in the refrigerator door, because the jarring movements of the door may lower the activity of the insulin. Try to keep your insulin on a low shelf in the refrigerator so it doesn't run the risk of freezing. Always examine your insulin before injecting it. Do not use insulin that is past the expiration date on the label and do not use insulin that is discolored or has clumps in it.

*C*an I reuse my syringes?

▼
TIP:

M any people reuse their syringes until the needles become dull. For most, this is safe and practical. However, the makers of disposable syringes recommend that syringes be thrown away after only one use. This is because after a syringe is used, there's no guarantee that's it's sterile. If you plan on reusing a syringe, keep these things in mind:

- Recap the syringe after each use.
- Throw away a syringe if the needle bends or becomes dull, or if you can't read the numbers on the side.
- Do not clean the needle with alcohol because this may remove the lubricant and make the next injection uncomfortable.
- Never use a syringe that has been used by someone else. You could possibly be infected with very dangerous illnesses (such as AIDS and hepatitis).

*W*hy do I feel tired all the time?

▼
TIP:

There could be lots of reasons. It could be a sign that your blood sugars are too high, or you're not getting enough exercise. Your heart may not be getting oxygen to your body correctly. It could also be a sign of depression. High blood sugars can make you feel very tired, and people with diabetes who are depressed are more likely to have high blood sugars. The more tired you are, the harder it is to take care of your diabetes. The combination of depression and poorly controlled diabetes can lead to a powerful sense of fatigue and loss of control. To break this cycle, work with your diabetes care team to get your blood sugars under control. Be patient. It may take several weeks for the effects of lowered blood sugar levels to provide you with more energy. Tell your diabetes care team your thoughts and feelings about being tired. If you improve your glucose control but still feel like you are failing and that nothing helps, you may be clinically depressed. Negative thinking makes you feel helpless. Counseling may help you learn how to change your thoughts, which may help your depression.

*W**hy do I keep having bladder infections?*

▼
TIP:

B ladder infections are common in women with diabetes. Unlike regular bladder infections, however, women with diabetes may not have pain or burning with urination, or bloody urine. These are called "asymptomatic" bladder infections (meaning there are no symptoms) and a recent study showed that 26% of women with diabetes had this type of bladder infection. Because there are no symptoms, only a urine test can tell you if you have an asymptomatic bladder infection.

These bladder infections probably occur because glucose in your urine provides a good place for bacteria to grow and your body's normal response to infection may be impaired because of your diabetes. Asymptomatic bladder infections are more common if you are older, have long-standing diabetes, spill large amounts of protein in your urine, or have had a bladder infection during the previous year. If your doctor prescribes medicine, be sure to follow the full course of treatment. If you notice a change in the color, concentration, or smell of your urine, you should talk to your diabetes care team.

Chapter 6
I CARE ABOUT NUTRITION

*I*s there a good way to figure out how
much carbohydrate is in a casserole?

▼

TIP:

If you are making a casserole at home, you can get a very good carb
count by adding up the carbohydrates in the ingredients and then
dividing the total carbohydrates by the number of servings. However,
this isn't going to work if you are eating at someone else's home or in
a restaurant. If you are eating a typical casserole (one with potatoes,
rice or noodles, meat, vegetables, and sauce), you can figure that each
1/2 cup of casserole has about 15 grams of carbohydrate (equal to one
fruit or bread exchange). This may not be exactly right, but it is a
close guess. Check your blood sugar two hours after eating the
casserole. If your blood sugar is higher than you expect, your
casserole probably had more carbohydrate calories than you guessed.
Either take more insulin or eat less casserole the next time.

*I*s there a simple way to know how much carbohydrate is in a homemade cookie?

TIP:

If you make the cookie yourself, you can add up the carbohydrates in the ingredients and divide that number by the number of cookies in the batch. Another way is to estimate based on the size of the cookie. On this page is a cookie meter. Place the cookie in the center of the ring and estimate its size.

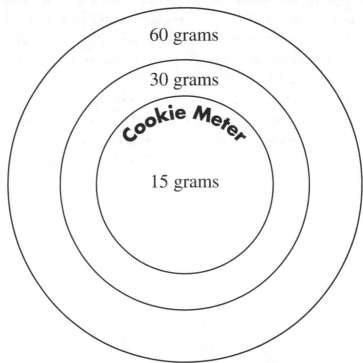

60 grams

30 grams

Cookie Meter

15 grams

*A*re sport drinks such as Gatorade okay for
people with diabetes?

▼
TIP:

Y es, but be careful. Some sport drinks have a lot of sugar and
could affect your blood glucose in nasty ways. Not having
enough fluid during or after exercise can lead to serious problems. So,
drinking plenty of fluids is very important. You should drink at least
2 quarts of fluid a day to avoid dehydration. Drinking an extra 4–8 oz
of fluid for each 30 minutes of intense exercise will help your body
achieve peak performance and recovery. Drinking something
other than water can add variety, but sport drinks contain about
15–20 grams of sugar and 50–70 calories per 8 oz, and the sugar is
often in the form of fructose corn syrup. Take the time to read labels
and compare ingredients, sugar, and carbohydrate amounts before
drinking these products. Always check blood sugar levels before and
after exercise. Listed below are some sport drinks and the grams of
sugar and calories for each.

Sport drink	Calories	Sugar/g
Allsport 8 oz	70	19 g
Gatorade 8 oz	50	14 g
Powerade 8 oz	70	15 g

*H*ow can I learn the carbohydrate and fat
content of fast food?

▼
TIP:

Fast food tends to be high in both fat and carbohydrate. However,
fast food can be included occasionally in a healthy diet. Most
national fast food chains have nutrition information available. All you
have to do is ask the manager. Sometimes this information is in the
form of exchanges, and sometimes it is given as grams per serving.

The ADA has an excellent book called *The American Diabetes
Association Guide to Healthy Restaurant Eating*, which lists information about food at popular fast food chains in the U.S. You can
buy it at *merchant.diabetes.org* or call (800) 232-6733 to get a free
catalog of ADA books.

*H*ow can I add fiber to my diet and
why should I?

▼
TIP:

W hen you eat a high carbohydrate meal with very little fiber,
your blood sugars may rise and then fall rapidly. Think of fiber
as a sponge, absorbing and then releasing sugar. A high-fiber meal
will slow down the rapid changes of blood sugar, preventing the
"highs and lows" you get with a high carbohydrate meal. The
National Institutes of Health recommends that adults eat 20–30 grams
of fiber per day.

Fiber can be found in many different types of plant foods,
including whole grain breads and cereals, fruits and vegetables, and
many types of beans. The best way to add fiber to your diet is to
slowly slip in more high-fiber foods. Add grated carrots, zucchini, or
celery to your usual meals. Use a handful of rolled oats to top
casseroles such as macaroni and cheese. Add garbanzo beans or
kidney beans to rice dishes. When baking cakes or cookies, use oat
flour for half the flour in the recipe and oat bran or oatmeal for the
other half to provide extra flavor and crunch. High-fiber foods are
low in fat and provide essential nutrients, such as vitamins C, B6,
A, E, folate, and carotenoids.

*W*here can I find current dietary guidelines for
healthy living?

▼
TIP:

In 1980, the Department of Agriculture and the Department of
Health and Human Services printed the first edition of *Dietary
Guidelines for Americans*. These guidelines are revised every 5 years
to keep up to date with advances in nutritional research. The
2000 edition gives 3 areas of specific recommendations for healthy
living.

1. **Aim for fitness:** Your goals should be to be physically active
   each day and maintain a healthy weight.
2. **Build a healthy base:** Let the food pyramid guide your food
   choices. Choose a variety of whole grains, fruits, and vegetables
   daily. Store foods properly to keep them fresh and safe to eat.
3. **Choose food sensibly:** Eat a diet low in saturated fat and cholesterol, and moderate in total fat. Drink low-calorie beverages.
   Prepare foods with less salt. If you drink alcoholic beverages, do
   so in moderation.

To get a full copy of the *Dietary Guidelines*, go to
www.health.gov/dietaryguidelines. Or write to the following
address: Consumer Information Center, Department 378-C,
Pueblo, CO 81009

*W*hat are omega-3 fatty acids and
should I include them in my diet?

▼
TIP:

Research has indicated that omega-3 fatty acids play a role in
healthier diets. These fats have a different chemical structure
then other fats. They improve "good" cholesterol (HDL) and improve
blood flow by making your blood cells less "sticky." Boosting
omega-3 fatty acids in your diet appears to cut the death rate if you
have had a heart attack, lowers the risk of various other heart
problems, lowers the risk of strokes, lowers triglyceride levels, and
slightly reduces blood pressure if you have high blood pressure.
Because foods high in omega-3 fatty acids tend to be high in fat, they
should replace other fatty foods in your diet. Omega-3 fatty acids can
be found in fish such as mackerel, herring, sardines, salmon, and
trout. The best plant sources for omega-3 fatty acids are tofu, soybean
oil, canola oil, and nuts. Fish oil supplements containing omega-3
fatty acids are also available, but it is better to eat a healthy diet than
to add supplements.

*I*s protein good for me?

No   Yes

▼
TIP:

I t is a popular belief that protein is good for your health. However, most Americans get more protein than they need. If 10% of your diet is protein, this is usually enough for your body's needs. Too much protein can damage your kidneys and add to kidney failure down the road. The best way to prevent kidney damage is to keep your sugar values as close to normal as you can, keep your blood pressure low, and eat a low-protein diet.

Protein is found in many foods but is particularly high in meat, dairy products, chicken, and eggs. Cutting down on protein has been shown to slow damage to kidney function in both type 1 and type 2 diabetes. Discuss with your diabetes care team what your kidney filtration rate is and whether a low protein diet would be good for your kidney's health.

*W*hat is a diabetic recipe?

▼
TIP:

G enerally speaking, there are no strict guidelines for a diabetic recipe. Most "diabetic" recipes just follow the American Diabetes Association nutrition guidelines and include diabetic exchanges. Also included is information on calories and the amount of carbohydrate in a serving. Many recipes use artificial sweeteners such as saccharin, aspartame, and acesulfame-K in place of part or all of the sugar. This helps keep the sugar levels down. However, even though less sugar is used, the final product may still have quite a bit of carbohydrate, especially if the recipe includes flour, milk, or fruit. When it comes to cooking, your main focus should be cutting down the carbohydrate, not just the sugar. Foods that used to be frowned upon because of sugar can now be worked into your meal plan. Remember, if you eat too much carbohydrate, you may cause a rise in your blood glucose. Always account for all of the carbohydrate you eat. Numerous books provide diabetic recipes. The bookstore on the ADA web site (*www.diabetes.org*) has available recipe books published by the American Diabetes Association.

*I*s there a simple way to estimate how
much I'm actually eating?

TIP:

O ne good idea is to use measuring cups as serving cups at home. If
you regularly use 1 cup, 1/2 cup, and 1/3 cup measuring cups to
serve your food, you can get very good at "eyeballing" the size of your
portions. The portions restaurants serve are often much larger than you
need. For example, a 1/3 cup of cooked rice has 15 grams of
carbohydrate and is equal to 1 bread exchange. However, you usually
get 2 full cups of rice in a restaurant, which is equal to 6 bread
exchanges. If you normally measure your rice portions using a
measuring cup at home, you can better judge a good amount of rice to
eat in a restaurant. Request a doggy bag at the beginning of your meal.
Take the extra food off your plate and you will be less tempted to eat
more than you need. The table below gives some examples of how
much food gives you 15 grams of carbohydrate for different foods.

Food	Amount	Carbohydrate grams	Servings/ exchanges
Popcorn	3 cups	15	1 bread
Mashed potatoes	1/2 cup	15	1 bread
Pinto beans	1/3 cup	15	1 bread
Strawberries, raw	1 1/4 cup	15	1 fruit
Cantaloupe, cubed	1 cup	15	1 fruit

*H*ow can I estimate how much salt is in my
food?

▼
TIP:

R ecommended salt intake for people with diabetes is the same as
for the rest of the population. To stay healthy, you should get
about 4 grams of salt per day (4,000 mg). Most food labels do not
give any information on salt content but do list "sodium" as one of
the ingredients (salt is made of sodium and chlorine). Sodium is the
part of salt that can be bad for your health, especially if you have high
blood pressure or heart problems. Four grams of salt contain 1,407
milligrams of sodium, which is equal to about one teaspoon.
Therefore, all you need is about one teaspoon of salt per day. This
sounds easy, but remember, many foods are soaked with sodium. You
should carefully read the sodium content on food labels (they'll be in
milligrams) and then convert it back into teaspoons of salt. What is
listed on the food label as sodium is less than half of the amount of
salt in that food. For example, if a can of soup contains 1,200
milligrams of sodium, then that equals approximately one-half
teaspoon of salt (2 grams). Four grams of salt a day is usually
included in a regular diet without adding table salt to any food.

*H*ow big is a serving?

TIP:

This is a tricky question to answer. Good nutrition comes in many different shapes and sizes, and suggested servings of foods and liquids may be difficult to figure out. The USDA Food Guide Pyramid gives a wide range of servings from each of the six major food groups. However, serving sizes are different within each group, and from group to group. Serving sizes are used to keep the level of calories, carbohydrates, protein, and fat the same within each group. When calories and carbohydrates are the same in your daily meal plan, then it's easier to keep your blood glucose stable. Following is a list of some serving sizes.

1 slice bread
1/2 cup cooked cereal
1/2 cup rice or pasta
1/3 cup cooked beans
1 cup milk or yogurt
1 oz cheese
1 cup raw vegetables
1/2 cup cooked vegetables
1/2 cup vegetable juice

1 medium size apple,
    banana, orange
1/2 cup fruit chopped,
    cooked, or canned in water
1/2–3/4 cup fruit juice
3 oz cooked beef, poultry, or
    fish
1 egg

A re soybeans good for me?

▼
TIP:

S ome studies have shown that soy may be good for you. Soybeans contain compounds called isoflavones, which are plant hormones that may be helpful in fighting problems like osteoporosis, certain cancers, and hot flashes during menopause. But soy's biggest strong point might be in how well it can lower cholesterol. At least 38 studies have found that people with high cholesterol levels who ate soy protein instead of animal protein lowered their total cholesterol, triglycerides, and LDL. The HDL ("good") cholesterol remained the same.

There are several ways to add soy to your diet. You can eat tofu, which is made from curdled soymilk. Tempeh is a formed cake made from fermented soybeans and has a firmer texture than tofu. Canned soybeans can be added to soups, stews, salads, etc. Soymilk makes great "smoothies." Now that soy is becoming accepted as a healthy food, soy products can be found just about everywhere. A good way to try some soy products is to go to the deli section of a health food store and ask for samples. You can also learn more about soy foods and how to prepare them by getting a good vegetarian cookbook.

*D*o sugar alcohols raise my blood glucose?

▼
TIP:

Yes, sugar alcohols can raise your blood sugar. Sugar alcohol is not the same as the alcohol found in alcoholic beverages. Many fruits and vegetables naturally contain sugar alcohols. Artificial sugar alcohols such as sorbitol, mannitol, and xylitol are often used as sweeteners and are classified as nutritive sweeteners. Nutritive sweeteners contain about 2 to 3 calories per gram instead of the 4 calories per gram you get from other carbohydrates. Because they still contain calories, sugar alcohols may affect your blood glucose levels and must be included in your meal plan. Other sweeteners (saccharin and aspartame) are not sugar alcohols and do not raise your blood sugar (they are calorie free). You should eat foods with sugar alcohols in moderation, since some sugar alcohols (sorbitol and mannitol) can have a laxative effect if you eat large amounts. Take time to read product labels, and become familiar with the food items in your grocery store that contain sugar alcohols.

*W*hy should I use a sugar substitute?

TIP:

In the past, people with diabetes used sugar substitutes because it was believed that eating sugar caused high blood glucose levels. Today, we know that sugars are just like any other carbohydrate and must be treated in the same way. However, by cutting down on sugar, you can seriously cut down on your total carbohydrates. Sodas, gelatin desserts, and chewing gums that are sugar-free will all contain less carbohydrate. All of the sweeteners listed here are calorie free.

Generic name	Brand name	How available	Notes
Aspartame	Nutrasweet	Many prepared foods	Loses flavor if heated
Saccharin	Sweet N Low	Many prepared foods— individual serving packets	Fine for cooking
Stevia	several	Pellets, at health food stores	Sold as a supplement, not approved as a food additive
Acesulfame K	Sunett	Many prepared foods	Fine for cooking

Chapter 7
BREAKING NEW GROUND—
DIABETES RESEARCH

*W*ill being in a clinical trial help my
diabetes?

▼
TIP:

Probably. No matter what, being in a clinical trial means you will
be examined more often than usual, which could lead to
problems being found earlier than they might have been. You may
also have the chance to test new therapies for diabetes. You should be
aware that if you take part, you might be given a placebo, or a
dummy pill with no real medication. It may surprise you, but many
patients actually get better even when they receive a dummy pill. This
is called a placebo effect. You may also receive the active treatment,
usually made up of a new medication of some type. Be aware that
new medications may have unknown side effects that are not
discovered until patients try the medications. But one thing is certain.
Before you participate in any clinical trial, you should read the
consent form very carefully and ask questions. If you are still
confused, bring the consent form home and go over it with a relative
or friend. Understand the consent form before you sign it.

*I*s there any way to improve my awareness of
low blood sugars?

TIP:

Most people with a blood sugar level less than 50 mg/dl suffer
from nervousness, shaking, sweating, hunger, difficulty
concentrating, and a rapid heart beat. Although these symptoms
sound terrible, having them tells you that you have low blood sugars
and allows you to correct them before something bad happens.
Unfortunately, not being able to notice your low blood sugars
(hypoglycemia unawareness) is common if you have long-standing
diabetes, especially in people with type 1 diabetes. This unawareness
is also common in people with very well-controlled blood sugars.

Usually, your health care providers will relax target blood glucose goals slightly if you lose your ability to notice your low blood
sugars. Avoiding hypoglycemia for a week or two will probably
improve your ability to sense a low blood sugar. Interestingly, a
recent study showed that people who took caffeine (equal to about
2 cups of coffee) had more frequent and more intense low blood
sugar symptoms than those that didn't. Thus, drinking two cups of
coffee every day may improve your ability to feel when your blood
sugar is getting low.

*W*hat do I need to know about
C-peptide?

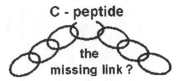

TIP:

When cells in the pancreas produce insulin, they also produce a
protein called C-peptide. C-peptide stands for "connecting
peptide." If you don't have diabetes, C-peptide is secreted with
insulin in equal amounts. Until recently, it was thought that C-peptide
didn't serve much of a purpose. However, recent studies seem to
suggest that daily injections of C-peptide may prevent kidney, bowel,
sexual, and circulatory complications in type 1 diabetes. People with
type 1 diabetes do not receive any C-peptide when they inject their
insulin because C-peptide is not included in their bottle of insulin. If
C-peptide proves to be helpful, it may be added to every insulin
bottle. Since C-peptide can be made commercially, this should give
us an additional tool for managing diabetes.

Because of the interest sparked by these first studies, new
research on C-peptide being added to insulin have been started in
both Europe and the United States. You will likely hear more about
this exciting development over the next several years.

*W*hen will there be a cure
for diabetes?

TIP:

No one knows the answer to your question because diabetes isn't just one disease. A more realistic question would be: "When will we have effective and safe treatments for diabetes?" Many effective treatments for chronic diseases are not cures at all. A good example is the treatment of hypothyroidism (low thyroid). There is no "cure" for hypothyroidism. However, the treatment (one thyroid pill per day) is simple, safe, effective, inexpensive, and completely erases the effects of the disease. If something like this were available for diabetes, the need for a "cure" could wait awhile.

The good news is that many new treatments for diabetes are becoming available each year. In just the last 5 years, diabetes treatment has come a long way. Unfortunately, many of these new treatments are expensive and have some pretty bad side effects. Right now, at least 35 new therapies for diabetes are being developed. The successful ones will not only be better than the treatments already available, but they'll probably lower the cost for all treatments due to competition in the marketplace.

Should I take estrogen after menopause?

▼
TIP:

This issue is still being debated. Taking estrogen prevents osteoporosis (when bones become weaker from aging) in women who take it regularly after menopause. It was also thought that estrogen prevented heart disease. Because women with diabetes are at a higher risk for heart disease, it seemed to make sense that women with diabetes should take estrogen after menopause. Recent studies, however, suggest something different. The Heart and Estrogen/Progestin Replacement Study showed that taking estrogen did not prevent the advancement of heart disease in women who already had heart disease when they started taking it. Because of this, experts are not sure whether or not they should prescribe estrogen for most of their female patients after menopause. Unfortunately, it is still not known if estrogen prevents heart disease in women who do not already have a history of heart disease. A national study is under way that will hopefully shed some light on this issue. Every woman with diabetes who has been through menopause should discuss the risks and benefits of estrogen therapy with their diabetes care team before making this important decision.

W^{hat is the HOPE Study?}

▼
TIP:

The major cause of death in people with diabetes is heart disease. It is 5 times more common in men with diabetes than in men without diabetes, and 10 times more common in women with diabetes than women without diabetes. Because of this, any treatment that will reduce the risk of heart disease in people with diabetes will save many lives. The HOPE Study was a very large study examining the effects of angiotensin-converting-enzyme inhibitors (or rampril, an ACE inhibitor medication) on lowering the death rate from heart attacks and strokes in high-risk patients. In the large group of 9,297 volunteers that were being studied, 3,577 had diabetes. Patients were randomly given either an ACE inhibitor or a placebo (a dummy pill) and then studied for 5 years. Because the ACE inhibitor worked so well in lowering heart attacks, stroke, and death from heart-related events, the study was stopped early. If you have any signs of kidney disease, ACE inhibitors can help because they slow the progression of this complication of diabetes. If you are not taking an ACE inhibitor, you should talk to your doctor about whether you should start.

IFG   IGT
Normal

*W*hat are impaired fasting glucose and impaired glucose tolerance?

TIP:

Impaired fasting glucose and impaired glucose tolerance are blood sugar levels that are higher than normal but not high enough to be diabetes. In the past, these conditions would have been called borderline diabetes.

If you have impaired fasting glucose and impaired glucose tolerance you're at a higher risk for type 2 diabetes. If you have impaired glucose tolerance you're also at a greater risk for heart disease. The treatment for either of these conditions is aerobic exercise and weight loss through meal planning. Resistance training (lifting weights) may also help by building your muscle mass. You and your doctor can decide on the best course of treatment. Below is a comparison between normal glucose values and the values of impaired fasting glucose or impaired glucose tolerance.

Normal	Impaired fasting glucose or impaired glucose tolerance
Fasting plasma glucose <110 mg/dl	Fasting plasma glucose ≥110 and <126 mg/dl (impaired fasting glucose)
Plasma glucose <140 mg/dl two hours after drinking 75 g of glucose	Plasma glucose ≥140 mg/dl two hours after drinking 75 g of glucose and <200 mg/dl (impaired glucose tolerance)

*W*ill an islet cell transplant cure my diabetes?

▼
TIP:

Y ou're not alone in looking toward islet cell transplant for hope. A recent study successfully transplanted islet cells in 7 patients with diabetes. After the transplant, the diabetes disappeared for at least 1 year. If longer-term trials go well, then islet cell transplant will be a major medical breakthrough. Before this happens, however, several questions need to be answered, including:

- How long will the transplant last?
- Will a second transplant (if needed) be as successful as the first transplant?
- Will the medications that prevent transplant rejection (when your body won't accept the new tissue) have any long-term side effects, such as cancer or kidney failure?
- Where will all the islets cells come from?
- How much will transplantation cost and who will pay for it?

As you can see, there's still a lot of research that needs to be done before we can properly answer your question.

*W*hat are the advantages of the new
blood glucose meters?

▼
TIP:

S everal new blood glucose meters are on the market, including the
Lifescan Ultra (LifeScan), the FreeStyle (Therasense), and AtLast
(Amira). These meters use less blood, are smaller and lighter (usually
the size of a credit card or shaped like a pen), give a reading within
15 seconds, and can draw blood from a variety of places, including
your forearm and thigh. If your life is hectic, a quicker meter may
make it easier to check your blood sugars more often, and a smaller
meter is easier to carry with you. Not having to prick your finger also
makes it a lot less painful. However, your insurance company may
not see the need for a different meter. Many insurance plans cover
only one brand of meter and strips. To get the strips for another meter,
your doctor or diabetes educator may need to write "a letter of
medical necessity" explaining why you need the new meter. Since the
new meters require a smaller blood sample, many insurance plans
will pay for your switch to another meter if you have calluses on your
fingers, which makes it hard to get a drop of blood.

*H*ow can I reduce hypoglycemia by
changing my pen injector technique?

TIP:

A recent study looked at 109 patients with diabetes who used pen injectors to see how well the NPH insulin in the pen was mixed before injection. The study found that the NPH insulin in the insulin cartridge had an unacceptable degree of variability in more than 70% of the patients. The study also found that by turning the pen upside down and then rightside up at least 20 times before you inject it could help this. This method works much better than just shaking the pen up and down. Low blood sugar was reduced among the patients who used this new method. This suggests that poorly mixed NPH insulin in injector pens can cause some attacks of unexpected low blood sugar. If you have not been mixing your cartridge insulin well enough, you may have fewer episodes of hypoglycemia when you mix your insulin this way.

*H*ow does my personality affect my blood sugar control?

▼
TIP:

It is likely that personality may play a part in how well you care for your diabetes. But which types of personalities will help and which won't? One recent study tried to answer this question. Detailed personality tests were given to 105 people with type 2 diabetes. The results of these tests were studied to see how well the personality of a person predicted their average blood sugar levels. Surprisingly, they found that people with personality traits such as anxiety, hostility, vulnerability, and self-consciousness usually had good diabetes control. On the other hand, people who had fewer negative emotions and a general focus on the needs of others were more likely to have poor diabetes control. This data suggests that people who are more focused on themselves are more likely to have good diabetes control than people who are not.

However, medical science is only starting to understand the relationship between personality and disease. More research is necessary before this information will become useful in your diabetes care.

*W*hy does diabetes nutrition news change?

▼
TIP:

It can be frustrating, but nutrition news changes as new information becomes available. Nutrition news is often based on research, which is usually based on one scientist's idea or theory. If it makes it through testing, the scientist's idea is thought to be well-founded—until another study is published with information saying something different. For example, early research suggested low-carb diets were best if you had diabetes. Now, it's recommended that carbohydrates be included in meal plans for a more balanced diet.

The problem is that separate studies are needed to answer a single question. Over time, all of the test results build a more complete picture of the truth. Unfortunately, the research results of one study are often presented to the public as the whole picture instead of just one piece of a larger picture. You might want to think of it as just one piece of a jigsaw puzzle. The next time you hear about "good" or "bad" diabetes nutrition news, remember that the information may be only a piece of the puzzle.

*W*hy did I gain weight after I started
  my new insulin sensitizer?

▼ TIP:

Insulin sensitizers are a powerful new class of type 2 diabetes drugs that work by lowering your insulin resistance. This category of diabetes medicines includes rosiglitazone (Avandia) and pioglitazone (Actos). Metformin also increases sensitivity to insulin but is not usually thought of as an "insulin sensitizer."

Insulin sensitizers have worked wonders for many people with type 2 diabetes. Unfortunately, you're probably also going to gain about 2 to 10 pounds when you use them. Part of this weight gain is from retained water, which may cause your shoes to be tight, make it difficult to get your rings on and off, and give you a feeling of tightness in your hands. This can usually be helped with a low dose of a diuretic medication. If you have a heart condition, be careful, because water retention can bring on congestive heart failure.

Studies have also shown that insulin sensitizers can increase your subcutaneous fat (the fat under your skin) and may result in a decrease in visceral fat (the fat around your midsection). Therefore, it is possible that these drugs move the fat from your stomach to the fat under your skin and that there is no real rise in total body fat.

Chapter 8
CUTTING THE RISKS

*W*ill drinking a little alcohol lower my risk of heart disease?

▼
TIP:

Recent newspaper and magazine articles have suggested that one alcoholic drink a day can help people without diabetes lower their risk for heart disease. Whether or not this applies to people with diabetes is still unclear. Recently, a study was conducted of 983 people with type 2 diabetes, including people who did not drink at all and people who drank one or more drinks per day. This test group was followed for 12 years, and it turned out that previous drinkers and people who did not drink at all had the highest death rate from heart disease. People who had at least one drink a day had the lowest death rate. Therefore, the answer is "Yes, alcohol does appear to reduce the risk of heart disease in people with diabetes." However, as you are probably aware, alcohol can have a lot of side effects, including hypoglycemia, alcohol addiction, and a worsening of blood fat levels. With this in mind, one drink per day with dinner is probably okay, but any more than that may be bad for your health.

*W*ill eggs increase my risk for
heart attack?

▼
TIP:

Egg yolks are very high in cholesterol, and many experts suggest lowering how much cholesterol you eat to reduce your risk of heart disease. A recent study of more than 117,000 men and women showed that eating up to one egg a day did not increase your risk for a heart attack or stroke—unless you have diabetes. For people with diabetes, eating one egg a day doubled the risk for a heart attack in men and raised the risk of heart attack in women by 50%. Instead of eating an egg, try eating an egg substitute, such as Egg Beaters®. Or, simply separate the white from the yolk and eat only the whites of your eggs. Although scrambled whites taste a little different than regular scrambled eggs, if you scramble 2 whites with 1 yolk every now and then, you probably won't be able to taste the difference. There is no cholesterol in egg whites, and by removing the yolks, you can halve your eggs and eat them too!

How can I help my child lose weight?

▼ TIP:

Right now, there is an epidemic of obesity in children and teenagers in this country. Because of this, there has also been a rise in type 2 diabetes at younger ages. Many studies show a high level of impaired glucose tolerance (pre-diabetes) and high fat levels in the blood of obese children. Since impaired glucose tolerance is a condition that leads to type 2 diabetes, you should have your child tested. This is especially important if you or others in your family already have type 2 diabetes.

The best way to help your child lose weight is to set an example of healthy eating and exercise. Include your child in family activities such as riding bicycles, hiking, or swimming. That way your child will not feel singled out and ashamed. If the whole family is living a healthy lifestyle, it is easier for the child to do it, too. The family can have fun setting goals, awarding prizes for accomplishing goals, and simply working together to prevent obesity and the risk of diabetes. If you make these changes and your child still fails to lose weight, you might consider seeing a specialist for help.

*H*ow low should my blood pressure be to prevent complications?

TIP:

The benefits you get from low blood pressure get better the lower your blood pressure goes. This is based on the recently completed, long-term United Kingdom Prospective Diabetes Study. This study, which lasted over 15 years, followed about 4,000 patients with type 2 diabetes and monitored how often they had diabetic complications. Besides showing that blood sugar control is important in stopping complications before they start, the results also showed the importance of blood pressure control. Almost every diabetic complication was linked with systolic high blood pressure (the top number of your blood pressure reading). In fact, for each 10 mmHg of lowered blood pressure, the risk of having any complication was reduced by at least 12%. Just like with blood glucose levels, the lower the blood pressure, the lower the risk of complications. With this in mind, your blood pressure should be as low as possible without causing you problems. Your target should be a blood pressure below 130/80. The bottom line—controlling your blood pressure is just as important as controlling your blood sugar.

A re high blood sugars after meals dangerous?

▼
TIP:

Y es, they are. As you know, high blood sugars can cause problems with your eyes, nerves, and kidneys. They may even put you at a higher risk for a heart attack. It is normal for your blood sugars to go up after a meal, but this can raise your average daily blood sugar. The perfect blood sugar after meals should be less than 150 mg/dl. There is a stronger relationship between your HbA1c and after-meal blood sugars than between HbA1c and your overnight fasting sugars. Since HbA1c is the measure of your long-term exposure to blood glucose, your blood sugars after meals may be the most important factor in your risk for diabetic complications. If you are interested in learning your blood sugar level after a meal, check your blood sugar level 2 hours after eating (when it is usually at its highest). Talk to your diabetes care team and develop treatment strategies to keep your meal-related sugars as normal as possible.

*W*hat is preconception counseling and why is it important?

▼ TIP:

I f you have diabetes, your chances of giving birth to a deformed baby are almost 5 times higher than if you didn't have diabetes. Preconception counseling can drop this risk down to normal levels. Preconception counseling is therapy for women who wish to become pregnant, and it can lower the risk of something going wrong with your pregnancy. There are 3 goals for preconception counseling:

- To achieve and maintain excellent glucose control before and during the pregnancy.
- To identify, evaluate, and treat complications of diabetes and risk factors that can have negative effects on you or your baby.
- To delay pregnancy until it is safe and wanted.

Unfortunately, preconception pregnancy counseling is not common in the United States. Many studies show that less than 25% of pregnant women with diabetes seek preconception counseling. If you are pregnant, or wish to become pregnant, and you have diabetes, do yourself and your baby a favor—cut the risk of something going wrong and seek preconception counseling.

*H*ow can I stop smoking?

▼
TIP:

The first step to a smoke-free lifestyle is realizing how horrible smoking is to your health. In fact, if you have diabetes, smoking is just about the worst thing you could do to your body. The thing is, you probably already know that smoking is bad for you, and you've probably already tried to quit more than once. By now you may think that your addiction to nicotine is so strong that you'll never be able to quit. But keep the following in mind:

- First, realize that many people have quit smoking who were just as addicted to nicotine as you are.
- Second, most people who quit smoking have tried to quit several times before they finally succeed.
- Third, trying to quit by yourself is very hard. Most people need help from outside support groups.
- Fourth, you'll probably get the best results by joining a behavioral modification program, combined with a nicotine patch and/or medications that lower you withdrawal symptoms.

Almost all communities have programs to help you quit smoking. Ask your diabetes care team what's available in your area. Quitting smoking is a long-term commitment. It is not easy to quit, but your health is worth the effort.

*W*hat can I do to prevent my child from getting type 2 diabetes?

TIP:

D iabetes is a growing health problem among American children. Until recently, almost all of the diabetes that occurred in children was type 1 diabetes. Type 2 diabetes in children was rare. Now, things are different. But why? More than likely it's because kids are getting less exercise and suffering from high rates of obesity. In order to prevent type 2 diabetes in your child:

- Do whatever possible to keep him or her thin.
- Limit how much time your child spends doing sedentary activities (like watching television or playing on the computer).
- Be aware of what and how much your child eats.
- Encourage your child to take part in lively, outdoor activities.
- Check age, height, and weight charts so you know how much your child should weigh compared to others of his/her age and height.
- Ask your diabetes care team to help you evaluate your child.

Remember, if you or other members of your family have type 2 diabetes, your child is at an even higher risk.

Chapter 9
MORE QUESTIONS, MORE ANSWERS

*W*ill acupuncture help the pain I have from neuropathy?

▼ TIP:

A lot of therapies can help you with the pain from neuropathy, including medications and improved blood glucose control. Recently, there's been a lot of talk about acupuncture, mostly from popular magazines on alternative therapies. As with all alternative therapies, it's hard to tell how well acupuncture really works. Many of the benefits could be linked to a "placebo effect," or benefits that don't necessarily come from the treatment itself but from the idea of being treated. Most of the studies on acupuncture have been done in China, but one study from the United States suggested that using acupuncture to treat diabetic neuropathy might be useful. Although we're still not sure how acupuncture works, it has been used to successfully treat pain in other conditions. More research is needed before we can say for certain that acupuncture is an effective way to treat pain from diabetic neuropathy. So before you start acupuncture therapy, talk with your diabetes care team about whether they think it's okay for you. If you decide to try acupuncture, don't stop using your regular medications. Remember that all treatments do not work the same for everyone, and acupuncture may help some people more than others.

*W**hy should I educate my friends about diabetes?***

▼
TIP:

When people don't understand something, they often feel uncomfortable or frightened. The best way to deal with this is to educate them. Tell them about diabetes—what is true and what is not true. For example, many people believe that you get diabetes from eating too much sugar, or that you can catch it from someone else. This, of course, is not true. Unfortunately, some people also think that type 2 diabetes is not a serious disease. Type 2 diabetes has many serious complications if you don't treat it right.

If you want to help, try lending your friends some books to read or show them *Diabetes Forecast.* If you are on insulin, explain hypoglycemia to them and show them exactly what they can do if you ever need help. Including others in your fight against diabetes can give you a valuable support group. Diabetes is much easier if you don't approach it alone. Most of all, show your friends by example that you can have diabetes and live a very normal life.

*C*an my computer help me with
   my diabetes?

▼
TIP:

The computer can be a big help in managing your diabetes. You can use it to track the food you eat, how much activity you get, and what your blood sugars are. Then you can use this information to get a better understanding of your diabetes data and make good management decisions. For example, you could compare how may calories you eat, how many calories you burn, and blood sugars over a six-month period. Using this information, you could make changes in your diet or activity plan to better meet your goals. Share your information with your diabetes care team so they can use your computer information to help you.

Several programs are available for people with diabetes. For example, *Lifeform* allows you to track calories, food composition, exercise, body weight, lab results, and how you feel each day. You can download a 21-day free trial from the website: *www.lifeform.com*. If you do not have your own computer, you can go to the public library and use their computers. Always keep in mind that computers are only as reliable as the information you give them. It's still up to you to review, adjust, and improve.

M *y diabetes is making me depressed. Will counseling help this?*

▼
TIP:

I f your doctor has suggested you get counseling for your depression, he may be worried about how you are feeling and what effect that might have on your diabetes. People get tired of dealing with a long-term illness like diabetes. They may begin to feel that there is no point in caring for their diabetes. It is important to find out what is causing or adding to your depression. Both professional counseling and medication can be helpful. People are often slow to ask for help because they think that they should be able to handle everything by themselves. However, at your first counseling visit, you will find that a good counselor is supportive and helpful. Counseling and/or medication for depression can be helpful tools for your diabetes management.

Who should I have on my diabetes care team?

TIP:

A diabetes care team is a group of health care professionals, friends, and family who focus on improving your health.

Primary group	Function
Primary care physician	Primary medical care
Dietitian	Healthy diet advice
Certified Diabetes Educator	Diabetes education and advice
Friends and family	Support and motivation
Dentist	Dental health
Pharmacist	Medication supply and advice
Secondary group	
Diabetologist	Endocrinologist specializing in in diabetes
Nephrologist	Kidney specialist
Neurologist	Nerve specialist
Ophthalmologist	Eye care and laser therapy
Podiatrist	Toe and foot care
Social worker	Financial advice
Mental health care professional	Psychological support
Exercise physiologist	Healthy exercise program

*H*ow can I contact other people
with diabetes?

▼
TIP:

I t's always a good idea to talk to other people who are dealing with
the same health problems that you are. Ask a diabetes educator if
there are any support groups or classes in your area that you could
attend. You might also ask friends and family if they know someone
who has diabetes. Another good way to contact people is the "Making
Friends" section of the ADA's *Diabetes Forecast* magazine. This is a
great way to get in touch with other people with similar problems. To
meet others through the magazine, write to:

Making Friends, ADA
1701 N. Beauregard Street
Alexandria, VA 22311

Young people can also use the web to meet others with diabetes.
Just go to *www.diabetes.org/wizdom*. Click into the "Make a Friend"
area to find a pen pal. Diabetes summer camp is also a great way for
children to meet each other.

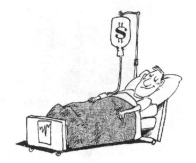

*W*hy won't my insurance company
pay for the diabetes supplies I
need?

▼
TIP:

S tudies have shown that preventing the complications from
diabetes is cheaper in the long run than getting the medical care
to treat them right. In fact, the two largest prospective studies for type
1 and type 2 diabetes (the Diabetes Control and Complications Trial
and the United Kingdom Prospective Diabetes Study) clearly showed
the money you can save with intensive diabetes management.
Unfortunately, the health care industry sees these savings as "future
savings," and not a way to save money in the here and now. When
health care plans are trying to save money in the short term, they
reduce how much they'll provide for diabetes expenses, and you
suffer. Even though this attitude is shortsighted, it is typical of most
insurance providers, especially Medicare and Medicaid, which are
run by the United States government. This is why it is very important
that you support the efforts of organizations such as the American
Diabetes Association. They are working hard to increase your health
care benefits. A reasonable health care policy that gives people with
diabetes proper medical supplies is urgently needed.

*S*hould I order my diabetes medication
through the mail?

▼
TIP:

If your medications and supplies stay about the same from month to month, mail order is a great way to go. For instance:

- Mail order pharmacies can deliver 2 to 3 months' worth of medication and supplies at a time.
- Prescriptions can be written for refills so that you automatically receive shipments every 30, 60, or 90 days.
- The items come directly to your door.
- Some mail order pharmacies can bill your insurance company directly.

However:

- If you need a drug quickly, mail order does not work well.
- If you prefer the personal attention you get at a local pharmacy, it's also not a good idea.
- Your order could get lost or delayed in the mail.
- If you are starting a new medication, you should buy it in person so you can ask your pharmacist questions. If you find that this new drug works for you and you will be on it for a while, mail order may be a good option.

Call your HMO or insurance company and ask if they have a mail order option.

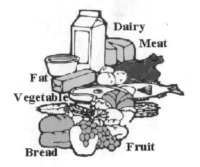

What is a meal plan?

TIP:

B asically, a meal plan is when you take time to think about a meal before you eat it. Sometimes meal planning happens 10 minutes before your next meal. Other times you can plan an entire week. No matter when it happens, an eating plan is an important part of diabetes therapy and can help you keep your blood sugars under control. A meal plan helps you manage the amount of carbohydrates and calories you take in on a daily basis. Meal planning is good if you have type 1 diabetes because you can match your insulin dose to the amount of carbohydrates you plan to eat. For type 2 diabetes, controlling the carbohydrates you take in can help keep your blood glucose in your target range. Meal plans can be developed to fit your tastes and your schedule, as well as your lifestyle. The USDA Food Guide Pyramid is a useful tool to develop a balanced meal plan. To make sure you and your family get the nutrients and fiber you need to stay healthy, choose foods from the 5 major food groups (bread, fruit, meat, dairy, and vegetable). Use as little as possible from the "fat" section. Take the time to develop a meal plan using the Food Guide Pyramid that will fit your lifestyle and that of your family.

*W*hy do I resist when my family tells me
what to eat?

▼
TIP:

Your family is probably worried about you and wants you to stay
healthy. Unfortunately, telling you what to eat is probably the
wrong way to approach the situation. It is a natural human response
to get defensive, especially if you feel you're being judged or
criticized. You may also feel guilt and shame from not sticking to
your meal plan, and this can cause you to resist as well. All of this is
normal. There is no evidence that having a family member hound you
all the time helps you improve your diabetes care. Only you can make
the decision to improve your dietary habits. However, your family
can encourage you. Think about what you would like your family to
say to you and tell them exactly what might help. Perhaps you don't
want to hear comments on what you eat. Ask them to stop bugging
you when you are not following your diet because that makes you
resentful. If you have a hard time talking to your family, talk to your
diabetes care team and see if they can help. A meeting between your
family and your diabetes care team may help them understand that
you are the one responsible for your diet.

I'm always afraid my diabetes care team is going to be upset with me if I don't meet my goals. Am I being silly?

TIP:

Your diabetes care team is not there to judge. They are there to help you get better control over your diabetes. Use them. The only way they can help is if you communicate. Still, it's common to worry about what your doctor might say. It can be very hard to change your lifestyle, especially if you need to lose weight and exercise. Many people struggle with lifestyle changes, and your diabetes care team knows that. It's easy to feel like there is something wrong with you when you can't "just do it." Unfortunately, this can cause you to avoid talking to the very people who can help you. Go to your appointment. Tell your doctor or another diabetes care team member what you're having trouble with. You may just need some help setting realistic goals. If members of your care team do get mad, you have the right to ask why. If it remains a problem, try and find professionals who won't judge or shame you. It's your life—you're the one in control.

*I*s it okay if my 11-year-old daughter with diabetes attends a friend's slumber party?

TIP:

Children with diabetes, and especially young teenagers, are often worried about being accepted by their friends. They want to be just like everyone else. By the time she's 11, your daughter may be taking on some of the responsibility for her diabetes care. If she hasn't started, now is a good time. Help your daughter take responsibility by making sure she understands what is needed and why. To best prepare her for her slumber party, make sure:

- she can take insulin without supervision
- she can check her blood glucose
- she can tell when she's having low blood sugar
- she has the snack she needs
- the parents of the child having the party are willing to help if she needs it
- you can be contacted if she needs anything

It is important for her to know that the better she manages her diabetes, the more like everyone else she will be. When both of you are comfortable about her diabetes management, you will feel better about letting her out into the world.

W*hy are the* Standards of Medical Care for Patients with Diabetes Mellitus *important to me?*

TIP:

T he *Standards*, published by the American Diabetes Association, are very important to your health and to other people with diabetes. These standards, or treatment guidelines, need to be followed by doctors, nurses, dietitians, and other health professionals who treat people with diabetes. They are often revised to stay up to date with the most current research in diabetes care. They are available on the web at *www.medscape.com/ADA/DC/1999/v22.s01/ dc22s01.01/toc-dc22s01.01.html* and in medical journals such as *Diabetes Care*. These guidelines describe the basics of acceptable medical therapy for patients with diabetes and include the tests that should be done during your annual physical, as well as other tests you should have. If you have a problem related to your diabetes, such as high blood fats, you should examine these standards to be sure that your healthcare team is doing what it should to get your levels in the healthy range. It is important that you understand what the goals of treatment are. By doing so, you can be sure you're getting good medical care. If your physician does not follow the *Standards*, we suggest changing to a physician who follows the *Standards of Medical Care for Patients with Diabetes Mellitus*.

Chapter 10
RESOURCES

Other 101 Tips Books

101 Tips for Staying Healthy with Diabetes. American Diabetes Association, 1999.

101 Tips for Improving Your Blood Sugar. American Diabetes Association, 1999.

101 Tips for Aging Well with Diabetes. American Diabetes Association, 2001.

101 Foot Care Tips for People with Diabetes. American Diabetes Association, 2000.

101 Nutrition Tips for People with Diabetes. American Diabetes Association, 1999.

101 Medication Tips for People with Diabetes. American Diabetes Association, 1999.

More Books by the American Diabetes Association

Complete Guide to Carb Counting. American Diabetes Association, 2001.

The "I Hate to Exercise" Book for People with Diabetes. American Diabetes Association, 2001.

Diabetes Meal Planning Made Easy. 2nd Edition, American Diabetes Association, 2000.

Diabetes A to Z. 4th Edition, American Diabetes Association, 2000.

American Diabetes Association Complete Guide to Diabetes. 2nd Edition, American Diabetes Association, 1999.

American Medical Association (312) 464-4818
515 North State Street
Chicago, IL 60610
www.ama-assn.org

American Association of Diabetes Educators (312) 644-2233
444 North Michigan Avenue, Suite 1240 (800) 832-6874
Chicago, IL 60611 (312) 644-4411 (fax)

The American Dietetic Association (312) 899-0040
216 West Jackson Boulevard, Suite 800 (800) 366-1655
Chicago, IL 60606 (312) 899-1979 (fax)

American Heart Association (800) 242-8721
7272 Greenville Avenue
Dallas, TX 75231
www.amhrt.org

Social Security Administration (800) 772-1213

Medicare Hotline (800) 638-6833

INDEX

Diabetes
  borderline, 81
  camp, 103
  contacting others with, 103
  cure, 78, 82
  education, 99
  medication via mail, 105
  nutrition, 86
  prevention in children, 96
  social interaction and, 109
  supplies, 104
Diabetes Control and Complication
  Trial, 104
Diabetes treatment plan, 15, 45
Diabetic recipe, 67
Dietary guidelines (*Dietary Guidelines
  for Americans*), 64
Diets, fad, 26
Diuretic, 19, 87
Driving, blood sugar levels during, 3

E
Eggs, 90
Endocrinologist, 4
Epinephrine, 7
Estrogen, 79
Exchange, food, 32, 31, 35, 59, 62, 68
Exercise, 42, 64
  aerobic, 37, 81
  benefits of, 39
  difficulty with, 40
  household chores as, 38
  lack of, 56, 91, 96
Eye examination, 46

F
Families First Program, 47
Family and Community Services, 47
Fast food, 23, 25
Fat
  body, 26
    subcutaneous, 87
    visceral, 87
  dietary, 25, 28, 30, 31, 34, 62, 64
Fatigue, 56
Fiber, 28, 35, 63

Food, portions, 22, 68, 70
Food pyramid, 64, 70, 106
Foot care, 48
Free foods, 22

G
Glucagon, 8
Glucose levels, 27, 39, 40, 92
  effects of personality on, 85
  during pregnancy, 94
  goals, 76
  while driving, 3

H
HbA1c, 45, 49, 93
Health Department, 47
Health Maintenance Organization
  (HMO), 49, 105
Heart
  attack, 11, 90, 93
  disease, 11, 28, 65, 79, 81, 87, 89
  rate, 37, 38
Hepatitis, 51, 55
  A, 50
  B, 50
High blood pressure. *See* Hypertension
High blood sugar. *See* Hyperglycemia
HIV, 51
HOPE study, 80
Humalog, 17
Human Services Department, 47
Hyperglycemia, 12, 56, 93
Hypertension, 39, 46, 65, 92
Hypoglycemia, 84, 89
  awareness, 76
    among friends, 99
  helping someone with, 8
  recovery from, 6
  unawareness, 2, 76
  while sleeping, 7
Hypothyroidism, 78

I
Impaired fasting glucose, 81
Impaired glucose tolerance, 81, 91
Influenza, 50

Sugar
  alcohols, 72
  dietary, 32
  substitutes, 73
Syringe
  disposal of, 51, 55
  reusing, 55

T
Triglycerides, 65, 71
Troglitazone, 19

U
United Kingdom Prospective Diabetes
  Study, 92, 104

V
Vaccinations, 50
Vegetarian, 33

W
Walking, 41
Weight gain
  from insulin, 12
  from insulin sensitizers, 87
  during the holidays, 27
Weight loss, 20, 22, 26, 28, 81
  in children, 91
Women, Infant, and Children Program,
  47

About the American Diabetes Association

The American Diabetes Association is the nation's leading voluntary health organization supporting diabetes research, information, and advocacy. Its mission is to prevent and cure diabetes and to improve the lives of all people affected by diabetes. The American Diabetes Association is the leading publisher of comprehensive diabetes information. Its huge library of practical and authoritative books for people with diabetes covers every aspect of self-care—cooking and nutrition, fitness, weight control, medications, complications, emotional issues, and general self-care.

To order American Diabetes Association books: Call 1-800-232-6733. Or log on to http://store.diabetes.org (Do not use www when typing in the web address.)

To join the American Diabetes Association: Call 1-800-806-7801. www.diabetes.org/membership

For more information about diabetes or ADA programs and services: Call 1-800-342-2383. E-mail: Customerservice@diabetes.org or log on to www.diabetes.org

To locate an ADA/NCQA Recognized Provider of quality diabetes care in your area: Call 1-703-549-1500 ext. 2202. www.diabetes.org/recognition/Physicians/ListAll.asp

To find an ADA Recognized Education Program in your area: Call 1-888-232-0822. www.diabetes.org/recognition/education.asp

To join the fight to increase funding for diabetes research, end discrimination, and improve insurance coverage: Call 1-800-342-2383. www.diabetes.org/advocacy

To find out how you can get involved with the programs in your community: Call 1-800-342-2383. See below for program Web addresses.

- *American Diabetes Month:* Educational activities aimed at those diagnosed with diabetes—month of November. www.diabetes.org/ADM
- *American Diabetes Alert:* Annual public awareness campaign to find the undiagnosed—held the fourth Tuesday in March. www.diabetes.org/alert
- *The Diabetes Assistance & Resources Program (DAR):* diabetes awareness program targeted to the Latino community. www.diabetes.org/DAR
- *African American Program:* diabetes awareness program targeted to the African American community. www.diabetes.org/africanamerican
- *Awakening the Spirit: Pathways to Diabetes Prevention & Control:* diabetes awareness program targeted to the Native American community. www.diabetes.org/awakening

To find out about an important research project regarding type 2 diabetes: www.diabetes.org/ada/research.asp

To obtain information on making a planned gift or charitable bequest: Call 1-888-700-7029. www.diabetes.org/ada/plan.asp

To make a donation or memorial contribution: Call 1-800-342-2383. www.diabetes.org/ada/cont.asp